One-Minute Mysteries & Brain Teasers

SANDY SILVERTHORNE
and JOHN WARNER

HARVEST HOUSE PUBLISHERS
EUGENE, OREGON

Cover by Dugan Design Group

Cover illustration © Sandy Silverthorne

ONE-MINUTE MYSTERIES AND BRAIN TEASERS
Copyright © 2007 by Sandy Silverthorne and John Warner
Published by Harvest House Publishers
Eugene, Oregon 97408
www.harvesthousepublishers.com

Library of Congress Cataloging-in-Publication Data
Silverthorne, Sandy
One-minute mysteries and brain teasers / Sandy Silverthorne and John Warner.
p. cm.
Includes index.
ISBN 978-0-7369-7396-0 (Choice Exclusive)
ISBN 978-0-7369-5472-3 (pbk.)
ISBN 978-0-7369-5473-0 (eBook)
1. Puzzles. 2. Detective and mystery stories. I. Warner, John., 1980- II Title.
GV1493.S585 2007
793.73—dc22

2007002500

Printed in the United States of America

22 23 24 25 / BP-SK / 10 9 8 7 6

To Katie and Ty—thank you for getting me
addicted to lateral thinking puzzles.
And to Kristin—thank you for your
encouragement and inspiration.

John

To Vicki and Christy—you constantly help
me figure out the mysteries of life.

Sandy

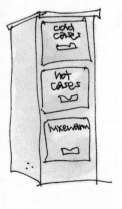

Thanks to Kristin Warner for
"Choosing Sides," "The Long Way
Home," "The New Girl," and
"Teacher's Pet." Thanks to Katie
Trimble for "What Is Your
Emergency?" and "Underpaid?"

Contents

INTRODUCTION

What Are One-Minute Mysteries?

These short mysteries, also known as lateral thinking puzzles, are often used in groups as an interactive game. Each puzzle describes an unusual scenario, and it is up to you and your friends to figure out what is going on. Although it is possible to come up with many answers that seem to solve the puzzle, the challenge is to find the solution that matches the one in the back of the book. Each mystery takes less than a minute to read, and then you can take your time and enjoy the sleuthing process.

How Do I Solve Them?

These puzzles do not provide you with enough information to find the solution, but you can fill in the gaps by asking yes-or-no questions. The process is similar to the game of 20 questions, but instead of finding the identity of a thing, you solve a mystery. You'll need one other person in order to enjoy these puzzles to the fullest, and the more people, the better! Choose one person to be the case master. This person reads a puzzle aloud and privately consults the answer in the back of the book. All other players are the detectives. They take turns posing questions to the case master, who can respond by saying yes or no or something like "That doesn't matter" or "Rephrase your question." The case master provides clues from the back of the book as needed. The game is won when someone figures out the key to the solution. It isn't necessary to recite the entire solution, but only to figure out the part that explains what is puzzling.

What Else Do I Need To Know?

Start by asking big-picture questions. You will be tempted to jump right in and guess the answer, but you will most likely be wrong. Give yourself something to build on by asking questions like these: Is the location important? Is anyone else involved? Could this happen to me? As you figure out what is going on, you can ask more specific questions. Also, ask completely random and off-the-wall questions. Think laterally—that is, think creatively or outside the box. If you have exhausted all the obvious possibilities and don't know where else to go, use your imagination and view the problem from a new perspective.

Eliminate red herrings and always check your assumptions. Look at each element of the puzzle and ask if it is important, and then focus on the details that matter. If a puzzle doesn't come right out and say something, don't assume it to be true. If the case master can't answer one of your questions with a yes or no but instead tells you to rephrase your question, you are probably assuming something.

If you decide to investigate these mysteries on your own, the clues section will serve as your guide. If you have a hunch of what the solution is, before looking at the answer, first examine the clues to see if you are on the right track. Some of the clues will surprise you! Once you have read all of the clues, your goal is to come up with a satisfying solution that fits all the constraints of the mystery and clues.

Oh—one last thing. Don't let the illustrations mislead you. They generally depict humorous but incorrect assumptions and are purely for your viewing enjoyment. Now put on your sleuthing caps and get on the case!

Shall we?

TIME TO THINK

1.

When Time Stands Still

As a burglar reaches for something on the mantel, he accidentally knocks over a clock. It falls to the floor, breaks, and stops. The next morning, however, police aren't able to determine what time the robbery took place. Why not?

2

Lunch Time

Robbie goes into a restaurant and orders a deli sandwich and a cola for lunch. Afterward, he pays his bill, tips his waitress, and goes outside. He slowly takes in his surroundings. The sky is black and the city streets are deserted.

What happened?

3.

Egg Timer

Hard-boiling an egg takes approximately ten minutes, but it isn't always as simple as that. Many factors can alter the time it takes. For example, in different parts of the world, hard-boiling an egg can take up to forty minutes. Why?

4.

Timeless

A man is looking at a clock that displays the correct time, but he doesn't know what time it is. Why not?

Got the Time?

Why does a secret agent check the time of day every time he finishes a phone call?

ON THE CASE

6.

Primary Evidence

James comes into his brother's room with his chest held high and a camera in hand. "I just got proof that the Benson twins are the ones who just TP'd our house," he gloats. John asks him a few questions and then says, "I'm sorry, bro, but you didn't get your proof." Why not?

The Hotel Guest

Charlotte knew two women were staying in the hotel room across the hall from her, but she had never seen or heard them. How did she know?

Women's Intuition

Julie peeked through the curtains when she heard a car pull into her driveway. She watched her husband get out of the car and walk toward the house. *I wonder where he's been?* she pondered. When Dave came inside, Julie welcomed him home. "What did you do today?" Dave asked. Julie described her afternoon, and before Dave could say anything, she said, "But I already know what you've been doing." How did she know?

9.

T-Shirt Trouble

Susan bought matching T-shirts for her and her young daughter, Sally. Later that week Sally walked into the kitchen wearing a shirt that fit her perfectly. Susan immediately knew that the shirt was actually the one she had bought for herself and that it had shrunk significantly. How did she know the shirt was her own and not the one she had bought for her daughter?

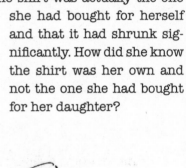

10.

The Missing Socks

Brian was determined to figure out why he had
a drawerful of mismatched socks. He knew
with a little detective work he would be able
to figure out why socks magically disappear
in the laundry. Eventually Brian did solve the
case of the missing socks. How did he do this
and what was going on?

11.

The Deductive Neighbor

Carrie's neighbors often go on elaborate trips around the world, so they do their best to make their home appear occupied to ward off burglars. Most of the time Carrie has no idea whether her neighbors are at home or out of the country. Even though Carrie hasn't seen or talked to her neighbors in months, recently she could tell whether they were in town or not. How did she know?

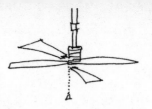

Lost and Found

Brad walked through the front door and almost
tripped over his wife. She was on her hands and
knees with her face inches from the floor. "Oh, Brad,"
she pouted. "The diamond fell out of my wedding
ring, and I lost it! I've been searching for hours! Our
house is so big, it could be anywhere!" Brad calmly
took her in his arms and told her it would be okay.
"I bet I'll find your diamond in the very first place I
look." How did he manage this when he
had no idea where the diamond was?

13.

The Hotel Thief

The Berkeley is a large turn-of-the-century hotel, favored by distinguished guests and people high in society. Recently a series of robberies has plagued the hotel, and Inspector Dublin, the local detective, was called in to investigate. Dublin rented a room and used himself as bait. He left his valuables on the dresser, and night after night he stayed awake and waited. One night, while dozing, a noise caught his attention. He switched on the bedside lamp and saw a thief frozen in surprise. After a quick struggle, Dublin subdued the culprit. Curiously, the Berkeley management decided not to notify the hotel guests of the capture. How come?

14.

Filthy Rich

While strolling along a city sidewalk, Lucas noticed a wallet submerged in a mud puddle. He carefully picked up the dirty and water-damaged wallet and was surprised to find it packed full of money. He didn't feel honest keeping it for himself, but the identification inside was unreadable. What did he do to find its rightful owner?

SLEEP ON IT

15.

The Early Bird

Mr. Baxter has a very important business
meeting early the next morning. He isn't
an early riser, so he checks and double-
checks his alarm clock to make sure he
won't accidentally oversleep. Later that
night while sleeping, he knocks over and
unplugs his clock, but the next morning he
wakes up on time anyway. Why?

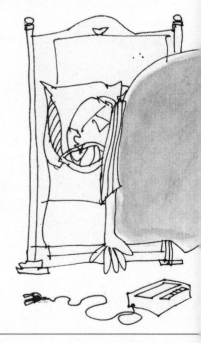

16.

The Failed Prank

Ben fell asleep long before his groomsmen. They decided to pull a prank on their bachelor friend, so they set the clocks forward so he would appear to have overslept and missed his wedding. The next morning, however, Ben immediately knew he had not overslept. Why?

17.

Siesta and Fiesta

Lisa was going to entertain some of her friends in the afternoon. After tidying the house and making some snacks, she had everything prepared 20 minutes early. Lisa felt a little worn-out and decided a short nap would restore her energy. But she didn't own any sort of alarm, and she didn't want to be asleep when her first guests arrived. Twenty minutes later Lisa felt fully refreshed and was greeting her guests as they arrived. Why?

great party, Lisa

18.

Unfamiliar Surroundings

Sam woke up disoriented and confused. He wasn't quite sure where he was. After a quick search of his immediate surroundings he found something that immediately reminded him of his whereabouts. What did he find?

19.

New Year's News

Jason Kennedy wakes up to the thud of the newspaper landing on his front porch. On his way to the door, he groans at the mess left over from his New Year's Eve party. Outside he opens the paper and reads the headline, "Jason Kennedy Wins New Year's Day Community Marathon." How could this be so?

20.

Sheepless in Seattle

George lay awake in bed for an hour while counting, but he couldn't fall asleep. How come?

21.

Rise and Shine...or Not

At 5:00 a.m. Ryan's alarm clock began its persistent droning. "That time already?" Ryan groaned as he smacked the clock. Trying to ignore the glow of the rising sun, Ryan pulled the covers over his head and fell asleep. He didn't wake up for a few hours. Why did Ryan set his alarm for 5:00 a.m. if he wasn't planning on getting up?

CALL ME
WITH THE
ANSWER

22.

First Date

Kati's friend set her up on a blind date with a guy named Chris. Being avid football fans, they decided to go to a game. Both had a wonderful time and agreed that they should go out again soon. The following day the phone rang in Kati's dorm room. She saw Chris' name on the caller ID but didn't answer the phone. Why not?

23.

Unknown Caller

Rex is surprised when the phone rings because he isn't expecting a phone call. He answers the phone and writes down a message. Oddly, he doesn't know the person who called or the person being called. He will never meet either of them. What is going on?

24.

Seven Digits

"I don't know his number," Jared said.

"Well, let me know when you find out," his mom replied.

Jared's friend was out of town on vacation, so Jared had no way of asking him for his phone number. Jared looked in the phone book, but the number was unlisted. Later, without any luck, he gave up. "Sorry I wasn't more helpful, Mom, but I still don't know his phone number."

"What are you talking about?" she asked. "You already gave me the number." How did that happen?

25.

What Is Your Emergency?

Susan decided to call one of her old friends during her lunch break, but when she called, a lady answered for the local emergency service. Why?

26.

Whom Shall I Say Is Calling?

A woman drops her kids off at school and then drives home. A few hours later she gets a phone call from her daughter but does not recognize the sound of her voice. Why not?

CRIMINAL
PUZZLEMENT

27.

A Dog's Life

As Billy opened the door, his dog,
Scruffy, made a run for it. *Great,
I'm going to be late for the bus
again.* Billy set his bag on the curb
and jogged after his runaway dog.
A few minutes later, with his dog
in his arms, Billy saw a man drive
up to his house, grab the bag, and
leave with it. Billy put his dog back
inside, and when his bus arrived, he
hopped on. What was going on?

28.

The Intruder

Jennifer lives alone and has the only set of keys to her house. Before she could enter her house, she knew someone was inside. She immediately called the police on her cell phone and reported an intruder. With no sign of forced entry, how did she know?

29.

In for Questioning

Sammy was a convicted bank robber who had strong mafia ties and many acquaintances in the crime underworld. One day, Sammy was seen on the location of a large bank heist. More than one person recognized him. Later, in police interrogation, Sammy lost his temper and threatened to use his connections. After many hours of questioning, Sammy left the station a free man and very pleased with himself. What had he done?

30.

The Tidy Crook

If the man had not been so tidy, he would have been successful in his crime. What happened?

31.

The Witty Cop

Wesley hunched in his unmarked police car and nursed a hot coffee. Multiple car thefts had occurred in the neighborhood, and he was on stakeout. Eventually a shady-looking fellow came sauntering down the sidewalk and paused beside a nice car. Wesley watched with growing amusement as the man jimmied the door open, hot-wired the car, and sped off. He'd caught the guy in the act! A few minutes later Wesley pulled the guy over and came up to the window.

"What seems to be the problem, officer?" the crook sneered.

Wesley gawked at the guy's nerve. Two could play at this game. He told the man he would be free to go if he could answer one question correctly. What question did Wesley ask?

32.

Robbed Again?

Nathan's house has been robbed numerous times,
but he knows for sure the robberies will end soon.
How come?

Sixth Sense

Ben is a clever con artist. He has led a group of scientists to believe he has special abilities. To test his special gifting they first place him in a room by himself and then suppress his regular five senses. During the test his abilities to see, hear, touch, smell, and taste are all blocked. At an unspecified time his assistant is sent into the room. Ben is miraculously able to tell when she enters. The scientists are baffled. How does he do it?

34.

The Unsafe Safe

Mr. Dunson was a very rich man who heard rumors that he was going to be robbed. In anticipation of the impending crime he decided to have his safe replaced with a newer model that was guaranteed to be impenetrable. One morning over coffee, Mr. Dunson suddenly realized he had made a mistake. Later, when entering his office, he saw that the safe was still closed, but he knew he had already been robbed. What happened?

35.

The Cheap Fix

A man's car has been broken into half a dozen times in the past few weeks. He loses money each time. After the owner purchases something that cost only a couple dollars, the break-ins cease completely. What did he buy?

36.

Joy Ride

Jim and his friends were going about 40 miles an hour in his boat when authorities stopped them and issued a citation. Jim wasn't speeding or breaking any water regulations, so what was going on?

37.

Quick Thinking

Benjamin works at a museum as a janitor. A few days ago he stole a collection of expensive crystal goblets and replaced them with cheap imitations. He then sold the originals on the black market for a small fortune. Even though the goblets in the museum are obviously fakes, he knows no one will suspect him of stealing the originals. How come?

38.

Above the Law?

A famous celebrity told some friends, "You know, I could go rob a bank, and everyone there would see it was me. The next day, all the newspapers and TV stations would announce that I'd robbed a bank, but I'd still get away with it." He was right. How come?

39.

Autograph Snatcher

A young boy received autographs from many of his favorite cartoon characters while on vacation with his family in Fun Land. He was so excited and so proud of them. Later a grown man came up to him and took the autographs away. What was going on?

Come back with those!

40.

Not So Safe

A man keeps his expensive belongings in safes. No one has ever seen him enter a combination, and he has never written one down or told it to anyone. When he opens one of his safes, he is shocked to find everything stolen. The safe wasn't damaged and had been locked, so how did the thief open the safe?

FOR THE ROAD

41.

Homeward Bound

Kimmy was on her way home for summer break after her yearlong foreign exchange program. The problem was that her parents had moved while she had been away. She was driving after dark into a confusing and crowded neighborhood, but her parents told her something that would make missing their house nearly impossible. What did they tell her?

42.

Running on Empty

Robert drove to the gas station and told the attendant to "fill 'er up." Afterward he drove off. Half an hour later he ran out of gas. What happened?

43.

Stuck in Traffic

Joe had an appointment he was eager to get to that afternoon right after work. Traffic was barely crawling due to road construction, and Joe sat impatiently in his truck for hours. Finally things cleared up, and he made it to his appointment. When he arrived, he saw that he was actually early. He wasn't able to leave work early, so how did this happen?

Choosing Sides

Austin left his house and drove to work on the right
side of the road. After work he drove home on the
left side of the road. Why?

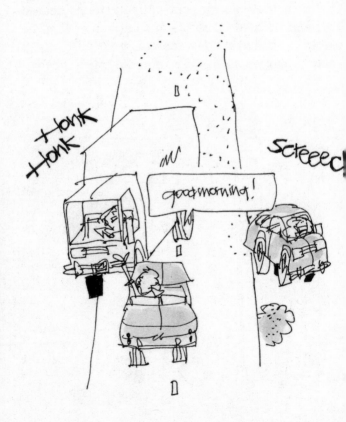

45.

Weather to Forget

A woman's car makes her more forgetful during the winter. How come?

46.

Seeing Is Believing

A man is nearly blind without his glasses, so when a gust of wind knocks them from his head, he is forced to pull his car over to the side of the road. Twenty minutes later he pulls back on the road and continues on his way. He couldn't find his glasses and didn't have any replacements, so how did he manage to drive?

47.

Pulled Over for No Reason?

As Frank drove down the interstate, he passed a police car parked on the side of the road. The cop pulled onto the freeway, came up behind Frank, and turned on his lights. Frank was a law-abiding citizen and was doing nothing wrong, so what was going on?

48.

The New Sound System

Adam recently had a brand-new stereo system installed in his truck. Why does he continue to listen to music on headphones?

49.

Fast-Food Freakishness

A man gets fast food every day for lunch. He prefers to use the drive-through because it's faster than going inside. But he only uses the drive-through when he has a passenger, and he always goes inside when he's alone. Why?

If you need me, I'll be inside

50.

Windshield Wipers Won't Work?

Why does a woman not use her windshield wipers even though it is raining and her car is getting wet?

51.

Green Light, Red Light

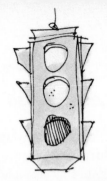

A traffic light in Syracuse, New York, has the green light positioned on top and the red light on the bottom. Its history stems from the 1930s, when Irish immigrants who moved to the area couldn't stand to see British red above Irish green, so they threw rocks at the traffic light. City officials grew tired of continually replacing the shattered red light and eventually decided to install a traffic light with green on top. Kevin, who is completely color blind and doesn't know this unique history, is approaching this very intersection. The blaring red light on the bottom of the traffic light appears to be green to his color-blind eyes. Kevin is driving by himself, and no other traffic is on the road, but he still comes to a complete stop. Why?

52.

Locked Road

Many old highways are gated so they can be closed during the winter when high snow levels make them inaccessible. Why did a forest ranger have a gate locked in the middle of the summer during the highway's busiest time of year?

53.

The Long Way Home

A man drives for three hours and ends up at home, but he did not drive to his house. What was going on?

FOR A PRICE

54.

The Inheritance

Bob was the only living relative of his recently deceased great-great-aunt. He arrives for the reading of the will, but afterward he's very displeased. Why?

55.

The Costly Item

While grocery shopping for her family, Shannon was having second thoughts about something she wanted to buy. She knew making the purchase was a mistake, but she did so nonetheless. It only cost her a couple dollars, but because of the purchase, she ended up having to pay thousands more. What did she buy?

56.

Two of a Kind

A woman comes across two ornate and expensive-looking boxes. They are priced the same. She spends a few minutes inspecting each one, and they look identical. She then deliberately buys one instead of the other. How come?

57.

Buyer's Remorse

While browsing through an antique shop, Tim found a very rare statue that made him very excited. He knew he absolutely had to have it, regardless of the price. After shelling out a small fortune, he drove home with his remarkable find. Later he became very upset over his purchase. The statue was authentic and worth everything he paid for it, so why was he upset?

58.

The Right Bank

James wasn't happy with his current bank. It didn't offer much security, it had a horrible interest rate, and its customer service was deplorable. He decided to withdraw all his funds and went straight to the first bank he could find. Even after all his hardships with his prior bank, he didn't bother to find out how this bank would compare. Why not?

59.

The Rare Book

A man owns a book worth thousands of dollars.
But every time the man even opens the book, it
decreases in value. He knows this is true and that
preserving it would be wise, but nonetheless he
continues to degrade its value. Why?

60.

One Person's Junk...

Derek decided to rid his house of a bunch of unwanted junk and have a yard sale. He put reasonable but substantial prices on everything. Things went quickly, and at the end of the sale, very few things remained. Still, he made very little money. Why?

that'll be 29¢

Yard Sale

61.

Underpaid?

A man works from 8:00 a.m. to 5:00 p.m. five days a week and only takes one hour off each day for his lunch. At the end of the week the man gets paid for only 35 hours of work. Why is this?

PUZZLING
BEHAVIOR

62.

Is It a Miracle?

A group of men are fishing all day in the middle of a lake. A man walks out to them, but no one seems surprised. Why not?

63.

Always Be Prepared

Brian cannot swim and avoids the water at all costs. Although he is usually never closer than five or six miles from any large bodies of water, Brian still keeps a life jacket close by most of the time. How come?

64.

Scared Silly

Suzie carefully steps through the dark and cluttered basement. Suddenly a rat scurries across her feet. She screams. Suzie then quickly picks up a bunch of mousetraps and throws them away. Why?

65.

If the Shoe Fits

Jenny has a pair of shoes that were given to her as a young girl, but she refuses to get rid of them and continues to wear them. Why?

66.

Trouble at Work

Karl enjoys his job and is a model employee. One day he drove to work, making sure to arrive early. He checked in with the front desk and then took care of a few other necessities. Things went well until suddenly he left more than an hour and a half early. No one told him he could leave, but he did so nonetheless. He was very angry and was overheard saying, "You won't see me in there again!" The next day, however, he showed up for work as though nothing had happened. What was going on?

I'm outta here!!!)

67.

That's Unheard Of

Why does a man who is completely deaf wear headphones that play loud music?

68.

A Passing Failure

A teacher gave a student an F on a homework assignment. After class, the student talked to her about it, and the teacher changed the grade to an A and even gave the student extra credit. What happened?

No Mulligan?

Thomas watched with pride as his ball soared through the air and came to rest within chipping distance of the green. He was in the zone today, more than halfway through the course and shooting significantly under par. Ten minutes later Thomas got out of his golf cart to find his ball. Even though Thomas had clearly seen where the ball had gone, he never found it and decided to go home without finishing the game. Why?

70.

For Sale Fib

Why does an extremely shy man put a For Sale sign in his front yard when he isn't planning to sell his house?

71.

Sudden Outburst

Leslie was calmly reading her book when suddenly her grandfather stuck his hands straight up and made a loud ruckus. Leslie completely ignored the interruption and continued reading as if nothing had happened. Her grandfather went back to sitting quietly. What was going on?

72.

What Not to Do

Sam and Devin don't like each other and never get along. But strangely, Sam always tells Devin his secrets and reveals his embarrassing moments. How come?

73.

The Forgotten Gift

"I'm so excited for the birthday party, Mom," Kevin chirped as his mom pulled their car into the Pizza-o-Rama parking lot. Kevin picked up the gift he'd bought for his friend Tim and locked it in the trunk before going inside. Why didn't he bring the present in with him to the party?

CLEVER
THINKERS

74.

A Needle in a Haystack

Mr. Riley recently conceded and purchased the solid gold hairpins his wife had been admiring. However, knowing his wife's tendency to lose things, he requested that she not wear the expensive jewelry while riding her horse.

Later, when her husband was away, Mrs. Riley caved in and wore the hairpins on her daily ride. The afternoon went flawlessly until, while putting away her horse, she snagged her hair on the saddle and lost her hairpin in a pile of hay. She was completely distraught because the long golden hairpin blended in perfectly with the straw. How did she find it?

It's got to be in here somewhere!

75.

A Key Solution

Betty loved going on runs with her dog each morning, but carrying her house keys with her was always a nuisance. Her running clothes didn't have pockets, and her husband didn't feel safe keeping a key hidden somewhere outside. She tried keeping a key tied around her neck, but it was too annoying. She hooked it to her dog's collar, but the key fell off and got lost. In the end Betty came up with a very clever alternative. What did she do?

76.

Who's There?

Darrel's grandmother lived alone and was tired of getting up and answering the door for salesmen and strangers, so she devised an easy method to screen her visitors. How did she do it?

77.

It's Not Polite to Stare

Sam may have initially been known as a nasally wuss, but his gaze won him many victories in the National Staring Contest. As one of the finalists and with the grand prize staring him in the face, he didn't plan on losing. The rules were simple: The first person to blink loses. How did Sam ensure his victory?

78.

All in a Name

"I saw your boyfriend, Aaron, today," Meagan smiled mischievously.

"My boyfriend?" Sharon paused. "I've never mentioned Aaron before, have I?"

Meagan took a sip of her coffee. "Never."

Sharon shook her head in disbelief. "Had you seen us together, or maybe a picture? How did you even know what he looked like? Did you talk to him?"

Meagan shrugged. "No, you've never told me about Aaron before, and neither has anyone else. I had no idea what he looked like, and no, I didn't talk to him. But even though you've never told me his name, his name told me he was your boyfriend."

How?

PUZZLING
SITUATIONS

79.

The New Girl

A girl from another country arrives in a town she
has never been to, but many people recognize and
know her. She doesn't seem surprised. The girl isn't
famous, so what is going on?

80.

Teacher's Pet

A teacher always calls
on the same girl first
when she raises her
hand. Why?

81.

Special Delivery

Every day Jack gets the mail, but one day
he gets something he was not expecting, and
therefore he never checks the mail again.
What does he get?

Playing Hooky

Carl frequently travels on business-related matters. On this particular trip, instead of going to the business meeting his employers expected him to attend, he went to the mall, to the movies, and to a nice restaurant, and he spent the rest of the afternoon at the pool. When his employers found out about his endeavors, they didn't fire him. Why not?

83.

All Trick and No Treat

On an unusually warm Halloween night, Susan read on the front porch while she waited for kids to come trick-or-treating. After many uneventful hours, she went to bed without one single trick-or-treater. What happened?

84.

Blind Date

Harold and Hannah met through an online dating service. They shared many interests and really liked one another. After months of e-mailing back and forth, they decided the time had come to meet in person. The day of their first date, Hannah e-mailed Harold a description of what she would be wearing. Later that day, both Harold and Hannah were in the appropriate places and really wanted to meet one another but didn't. Why not?

85.

The Invisible Girl

Freddie and Carly go to school together and enjoy playing hide-and-seek during recess. Freddie was never too hard to find, but when Carly hid, Freddie never found her. Why?

86.

More or Less?

What can either grow larger or completely disappear due to the same action?

Fleeting Interest

Frank was very anxious to go to the library and get a particular book. When he arrived, he went straight to a particular shelf and scanned the titles. Not finding the book, he searched the computer database to see if the book had been checked out already. Frank was very discouraged when he saw that the book was indeed in circulation and wouldn't be back for two weeks. Frank never ended up getting the book. Why did he lose interest?

88.

Art for the Ages

As a young woman traveling in Italy, Jane bought some artwork she was fond of. Throughout the years she kept it with her as she moved from house to house. Many of her friends and family admired it, but when she passed away as an old woman, she had it buried with her instead of leaving it to anyone. Why?

89.

Losing with Style

Charles ran a race in the
fastest time but didn't win
first place. Why not?

90.

Mirror, Mirror

When can you look in a mirror
but not see your reflection?

91.

Puzzle Puzzle

Simon was putting together a jigsaw puzzle. Strangely, he had no idea what the image was until he placed the final puzzle piece. How can that be?

92.

Artistic License

If a woman has never seen her own face, how can she paint a very accurate self-portrait?

93.

The House Painter

After getting laid off for the summer, Jim had a lot of time on his hands, so he focused on some projects around the house. A neighbor came by one day while Jim was painting his house. Impressed with Jim's work, the neighbor hired him to do his house also. One thing led to another, and Jim spent the next 30 years as a house painter, but he never left his small suburban neighborhood to do so. How could that be?

94.

Water Rules

Leon isn't a little kid, but he isn't allowed in the pool by himself. How come?

95.

Lucky Bug

A bug flew into a man's eye, and because of that, the man got a date. Why?

96.

Power Outage

A man arrives home late one night after work. He flips on the lights and heats up some leftovers. He enjoys his meal in front of the heater while listening to jazz on the radio. Afterward he takes a nice long hot shower. At 11:30 he decides to watch the evening news, but the TV will not turn on. He shrugs. "Oh well, the power must still be out." What is going on?

97.

A Case of Amnesia?

After a traumatic experience, James opened his eyes in a hospital. He didn't know who he was or what his name was. People calling themselves his family were there, but he didn't recognize any of them. Things were never the same for him, but he adjusted to a new life. He never remembered his life from before and never talked about it. What had happened?

Good Advice

A man has a habit of losing his
stuff. His friends make suggestions
to help him, but nothing works.
Eventually one of his closer friends
recommends something that will
certainly solve his problem. He
takes his advice, and it works.
What was the advice?

99.

Bad Hair Day

James has had his hair cut the same way for the past ten years. His friends tell him to do something new, but when he does, James becomes very distraught. Why?

100.

When It Rains, It Pours

Tom Baker wakes up to the sound of rain on his bedroom window. A few minutes later, after a mad rush of getting ready and pulling his rain gear out of storage, he is in the garage, starting his car. He had overslept again and is late for work. Tom then realizes the remote garage door opener is still on the kitchen counter. He hops out of the car and pulls on the door but finds it locked. Turning around, he tries to get into his car, but it's locked too! There is no other way to open the garage door other than with the remote, so what does he do?

CLUES

TIME TO THINK

1. When Time Stands Still
- The police could see the clock.
- The burglar did not alter the clock in any way after it fell.
- The police didn't expect to be able to read the clock.
- What kind of clock is it?

2. Lunch Time
- Nothing supernatural happened.
- The man was on his lunch break.
- It was like this before he went to lunch.
- What time is it?

3. Egg Timer
- Elevation doesn't matter in this case.
- Outdoor temperature doesn't matter in this case.
- What other factors affect cooking time?
- What kind of bird are you assuming the egg came from?

4. Timeless
- The man can see and tell time perfectly well.
- The clock is normal and in plain sight.
- More than one clock is in the room.

5. **Got the Time?**

- He doesn't care what time it is.
- He doesn't use his watch to check the time.
- He is covering his tracks.
- He doesn't want people to know whom he called.

ON THE CASE

6. **Primary Evidence**

- The camera has film in it.
- John asked his brother where he was when he took the picture.
- It was dark outside.
- James ended up with a picture of himself.

7. **The Hotel Guest**

- She didn't hear anything.
- She didn't see anything being taken into the hotel room.
- She figured this out in the morning.
- The women had room service for breakfast.

8. **Women's Intuition**

- Dave's clothing is not relevant.
- Dave does this often.
- Julie figured it out as she kissed Dave.
- His breath smelled normal.

9. **T-Shirt Trouble**

- The shirts she bought were identical in every way except for the size.
- Nothing changed about her shirt except its size.
- Sally was carrying her own shirt.

10. **The Missing Socks**
- Only brightly colored socks were missing.
- Brian discovered that the missing socks were stolen.
- The dryer was broken.

11. **The Deductive Neighbor**
- Carrie never saw anyone enter or leave the house (including pets!).
- She couldn't tell whether her neighbors were home during the summer.
- She saw something coming out of the house.

12. **Lost and Found**
- Brad took a while to find the diamond, but it was in the first place he looked.
- He found the diamond in a different place from where it was lost.
- Brad's wife dropped the ring on the carpet.
- Brad did one of his chores before finding the ring.

13. **The Hotel Thief**
- The thief lives at the hotel.
- They didn't want to reveal the culprit.
- Revealing the culprit would do more harm than good.
- The thief couldn't talk.

14. **Filthy Rich**
- Something is different about the money.
- Check your assumptions on why the ID was unreadable.
- Lucas lives in a big city on the eastern coast of the United States.

SLEEP ON IT

15. **The Early Bird**
- It was still dark when he woke up.
- A sound didn't wake him up.
- He knew he would be tired in the morning so he planned ahead.
- He smelled something.

16. **The Failed Prank**
- Ben was not aware of the prank.
- Every clock in the room was changed.
- The alarm was reset so they wouldn't actually oversleep.
- It was a clock radio.

17. **Siesta and Fiesta**
- A sound woke her up.
- It wasn't the doorbell.
- The sound came from something significant to the party.
- She served crumpets at her party.

18. **Unfamiliar Surroundings**
- He was alone in the room.
- Sam had never been in this room before.
- The answer could be found in a Bible.

19. **New Year's News**
- Jason stayed up all night partying.
- The newspaper was that day's edition.
- The paper came at the normal time.
- Jason was awakened from a nap.

20. Sheepless in Seattle

- George was tired and wanted to fall asleep.
- George wasn't counting to help himself fall asleep.
- George was counting something that kept him awake.
- It was raining.

21. Rise and Shine...or Not

- His alarm was set so he would do something.
- It didn't involve getting out of bed.
- He didn't need to be awake at 5:00 a.m.
- The alarm didn't wake him up.

CALL ME WITH THE ANSWER

22. First Date

- Kati really did like Chris.
- Kati had a good reason for not answering the phone.
- Kati and Chris were both enthusiastic fans.
- Kati couldn't answer the phone.

23. Unknown Caller

- Rex was at work.
- He was in a public place.
- It wasn't his personal phone.

24. Seven Digits

- Jared never found the phone number.
- Why would Jared's mom need a phone number for a friend who is out of town?
- Jared was talking to his mom on the phone.

25. **What Is Your Emergency?**
- Susan's friend didn't work for the emergency service.
- Susan accidentally called 911.
- Susan was calling from work.

26. **Whom Shall I Say Is Calling?**
- Nothing is wrong with her daughter's voice.
- She has never heard her daughter speak.
- She didn't drop her daughter off at school that morning.

CRIMINAL PUZZLEMENT

27. **A Dog's Life**
- The man is a stranger.
- Scruffy escaping is irrelevant.
- This happens every week.

28. **The Intruder**
- The front door is the only way into the house.
- One thing was different with the door.
- She couldn't have done this herself.
- She couldn't enter her house.

29. **In for Questioning**
- Sammy was innocent.
- He showed up after the crime was committed.
- Someone else was convicted through the interrogation.

30. **The Tidy Crook**
- Being messy would have made him successful.

- What he stole was not worth much money but did have value.
- Something didn't happen that he wanted to happen.
- The crook left a ransom note.

31. **The Witty Cop**
- Wesley didn't know the answer to his own question.
- Only the owner of the car would know the answer.
- The answer could be easily attained.
- Something with the radio.

32. **Robbed Again?**
- He is not waiting on any type of surveillance.
- The house is not broken into.
- No one currently lives in the house.
- It is really easy to enter.

33. **Sixth Sense**
- The assistant is in on the deception.
- There is something about his assistant that he can sense.
- Ben cannot smell but he can still breathe.

34. **The Unsafe Safe**
- The installation of the new safe isn't relevant to the crime.
- He knew he had been robbed because he could see his safe.
- The thief didn't know about the safe until after the crime.
- He has a wall safe.

35. **The Cheap Fix**
- He bought a container.
- He knows the person breaking into his car.
- Money isn't stolen.

36. **Joy Ride**
- Jim had all necessary permits, licenses, and equipment.
- Under these circumstances, he didn't need life jackets.
- No one was driving the boat.
- The boat was being pulled.

37. **Quick Thinking**
- The goblets are not revealed as fakes.
- The goblets are never examined.
- Benjamin is fired.

38. **Above the Law?**
- There is no loophole; he would be breaking the law.
- His celebrity status is important.
- People wouldn't know who he was.
- This may happen at Halloween.

39. **Autograph Snatcher**
- The boy kept his autographs with him at all times.
- The boy was scared at first but happy afterward.
- The autographs were returned to the boy.
- Afterward the boy no longer kept the autographs with him at all times.

40. **Not So Safe**
- The thief didn't have any special knowledge in breaking into safes.
- The man had a terrible memory.
- The thief didn't need a combination.

FOR THE ROAD

41. Homeward Bound
- Something about the house was unique.
- This difference could be seen in the dark.
- It would not be unusual at a different time of year.

42. Running on Empty
- Robert only drove a few miles.
- The tank didn't leak.
- He wasn't driving when he ran out of gas.

43. Stuck in Traffic
- Joe knew he'd encounter road construction.
- He didn't expect the road construction to make him late to the appointment.
- Joe took only a few minutes to drive to his appointment.
- What does Joe do for work?

44. Choosing Sides
- Austin didn't encounter any construction.
- He is doing the right thing.
- He doesn't live in America.

45. Weather to Forget
- She is forgetful while getting into her car.
- It has to do with where she leaves things.
- The type of car is important.
- She drives a convertible.

46. **Seeing Is Believing**
- He could see perfectly well.
- He didn't have surgery.
- His blindness was only temporary.
- It was early evening.

47. **Pulled Over for No Reason?**
- The police officer didn't pass Frank.
- The police officer had a good reason to turn on his lights.
- Frank didn't pull over. Actually, he never even considered it!
- There was a beautiful sunset.

48. **The New Sound System**
- Adam drives alone.
- The stereo system is in perfect working order.
- Adam drives for a job.
- The stereo is in use.

49. **Fast Food Freakishness**
- When he's alone, going inside is easier than using the drive-through.
- The man's car is unique.
- It's a foreign car.

50. **Windshield Wipers Won't Work?**
- The windshield wipers are in working order.
- The car is on and moving.
- Rain isn't falling on her car.
- The car is in neutral.

51. **Green Light, Red Light**
- The intersection has no signs or warnings.
- Kevin is confused.
- Nothing but the traffic light is relevant.

52. **Locked Road**
- The highway was safe for travel.
- The gate was locked *because* it was the busy season.
- People still traveled on the highway.
- The road wasn't blocked.

53. **The Long Way Home**
- He wasn't driving a motor home.
- He does this often for fun.
- He never left his house.

FOR A PRICE

54. **The Inheritance**
- Bob's aunt was very rich and left everything to him.
- Bob left empty-handed.
- His aunt didn't die of old age.

55. **The Costly Item**
- Nothing illegal was happening.
- The purchase was not related to her health.
- She wasn't upset.
- She was very lucky.

56. **Two of a Kind**
- Both are genuine.
- Neither box has a flaw.
- The boxes are *visually* identical.

57. **Buyer's Remorse**
- He was happy to have the statue.
- He became upset when he put the statue with his collection.
- He already had a spot for the statue.

58. **The Right Bank**
- James knew nothing about the new bank.
- James wasn't acting foolhardily.
- His old bank had a very small clientele.

59. **The Rare Book**
- Its value decreases and increases.
- The book isn't old.
- The book is easily replaced.
- He writes in the book.

60. **One Person's Junk...**
- Nothing was stolen.
- He didn't change any prices.
- Nothing was given away.
- He sold very little.

61. **Underpaid?**
- The man gets paid for every hour he works.
- Lunch time isn't all about food.
- The man works two jobs.
- One of his jobs is in another state.

PUZZLING BEHAVIOR

62. Is It a Miracle?
- The man was not Jesus.
- The men were not in a boat.
- The season is important.

63. Always Be Prepared
- Brian is a completely normal human adult.
- Think of the miles in terms of feet.
- The life jacket is mandatory.
- What does Brian do for work?

64. Scared Silly
- The mousetraps were empty.
- Her behavior wasn't unusual.
- She screamed because she was startled but not scared.

65. If the Shoe Fits
- The shoes are too small for her feet.
- The shoes don't cause her any pain.
- Sometimes she wears two pairs of shoes.
- The shoes are gold.

66. Trouble at Work
- Something Karl saw made him angry.
- He wasn't scheduled to work that day.
- He brought his family.
- Where does Karl work?

67. That's Unheard Of
- He only does this in public places.

- If he is with a friend, he doesn't wear the headphones.
- He can read lips and speaks normally.
- People wearing headphones that blast music cannot hear anything else.

68. A Passing Failure

- The paper was A-quality work.
- The student received extra credit for the same thing that originally gave her an F.
- The paper was written utilizing something in the paper's topic.
- The teacher couldn't read the paper without help.

69. No Mulligan?

- The golf ball was in plain sight and still in play.
- Something happened that made it very hard to play golf.
- Thomas took only three minutes to drive from the tee to the green.
- So why did Thomas stay under the golf cart for seven extra minutes?

70. For Sale Fib

- He wants someone to think he is moving.
- He wants something to be done without asking for it.
- He wants his neighbor to think he's moving, but why?
- The neighbor has something the man wants.

71. Sudden Outburst

- Leslie's grandfather wasn't watching any sports.
- Leslie wasn't surprised by the outburst.
- This happens every day.
- It happens at the same time each day.

72. **What Not to Do**
- Sam isn't forced into telling these things.
- Sam doesn't know he's telling his secrets.
- They have known each other all their lives.

73. **The Forgotten Gift**
- Everyone else had brought gifts into the pizza parlor.
- Kevin never brought the gift into the pizza parlor.
- Tim wasn't at the party.

CLEVER THINKERS

74. **A Needle in a Haystack**
- She didn't burn the hay.
- She used something that was readily available.
- She didn't use her horse.
- The hairpins were heavier than the pieces of hay.

75. **A Key Solution**
- Betty didn't take a key with her or leave one in an unsafe place.
- The key was in a place that a burglar couldn't get to.
- The key was in a place that Betty couldn't get to.
- Betty's dog was very obedient.

76. **Who's There?**
- She didn't spend any money.
- She still answered the door for friends and family.
- Friends and family did something different than strangers did.
- Her solution was simpler than a secret knock.

77. **It's Not Polite to Stare**
- He cheated.
- He had plugs in his nose.
- He made his opponent close his eyes.

78. **All in a Name**
- Aaron didn't have his name on him.
- Sharon had her boyfriend's name on her.
- Aaron had Sharon's name on him.
- The name was in a heart.

PUZZLING SITUATIONS

79. **The New Girl**
- None of the people have seen her before.
- The girl has a good reason to visit.
- She is mistaken for someone else.

80. **Teacher's Pet**
- Raising her hand isn't mandatory.
- The girl knows the teacher very well.
- She only has one teacher.

81. **Special Delivery**
- What he got didn't come in the mail.
- He couldn't physically check the mail anymore.
- He wasn't an honest man.

82. **Playing Hooky**
- His employers were indeed upset.
- Carl was still doing his job.

- Someone else got in trouble.
- What is Carl's job?

83. **All Trick and No Treat**
- Kids went trick-or-treating at every other house in the neighborhood.
- Susan was a perfectly kind woman, and kids loved her.
- Something happened that Susan didn't notice.
- Kids thought she wasn't home.

84. **Blind Date**
- They planned to meet at Harold's work.
- Something was wrong with the description Hannah provided.
- Harold wasn't able to distinguish who she was.
- Harold is a security guard.

85. **The Invisible Girl**
- Carly is a real girl.
- She was cheating.
- He could never go where she was hiding.

86. **More or Less?**
- A person performs the action.
- Once it grows too large, the same action will no longer make it disappear.
- This may happen while camping.

87. **Fleeting Interest**
- Frank wasn't looking for the book in order to read it.
- How did he know where the book belonged?
- He had read the book before.

88. **Art for the Ages**

- Buying the art in Italy isn't relevant.
- The artwork was small.
- At one point in her life she didn't like the artwork but kept it anyway.

89. **Losing with Style**

- Charles was a normal human athlete.
- Other athletes finished the race before he did.
- He would have won first place in different circumstances.

90. **Mirror, Mirror**

- The answer has nothing to do with one-way mirrors, double mirrors, or anything magical.
- You don't see any reflection at all.
- Think about looking in something other than just the glass of a mirror.

91. **Puzzle Puzzle**

- Simon had his eyes open.
- It was a normal jigsaw puzzle.
- Simon's method of assembling the puzzle was very challenging.

92. **Artistic License**

- She is not blind.
- She doesn't receive any verbal instruction.
- It isn't really a self-portrait but it looks like one.
- She has siblings.

93. **The House Painter**

- Jim never painted the same house more than once.
- Jim painted thousands of houses.

- Jim painted houses from all over the world.
- Many of the houses Jim painted didn't exist.

94. **Water Rules**
- Leon is a fully normal adult human.
- No water is in the pool.
- At least one other person must be in the pool with Leon.
- It isn't a swimming pool.

95. **Lucky Bug**
- A woman was watching the man.
- The woman didn't know a bug had flown into the man's eye.

96. **Power Outage**
- The power has been out all day.
- The man lives in the country.

97. **A Case of Amnesia?**
- James wasn't in an accident, didn't suffer an injury, and didn't have amnesia.
- James had never seen these people before.
- James didn't know his name because he'd never heard it before.

98. **Good Advice**
- If it isn't nailed down, this man can lose it.
- His friends don't necessarily want him to stop losing his stuff.
- The advice he took required a lifestyle change.
- His friends benefit from his loss.

99. **Bad Hair Day**
- James doesn't get his hair cut in a new way.

- James tries growing his hair longer.
- James is an older man.

100. **When It Rains, It Pours**
- Nothing is broken in the process.
- It wasn't raining the day before.
- The keys are easily attained.

SOLUTIONS

TIME TO THINK

1. **When Time Stands Still**
   The burglar knocked over a digital clock. When it broke and stopped, it no longer displayed the time.

2. **Lunch Time**
   The man worked the night shift and took his lunch break in the middle of the night.

3. **Egg Timer**
   Some eggs are larger than others. Ostrich eggs can weigh three to six pounds and can take between 45 minutes and two hours to hard-boil. One ostrich egg is equivalent to two dozen chicken eggs.

4. **Timeless**
   Each clock in the room is displaying a different time, so he doesn't know which one is correct.

5. **Got the Time?**
   The secret agent calls the phone number for the current time, which replaces the redial memory on the phone so that no one can find out whom he was calling.

ON THE CASE

6. **Primary Evidence**
James took the photo from inside the house, and the camera flash reflected off a dark window, which acted as a mirror. The Benson twins were never caught in the act, and James ended up with a photo of himself.

7. **The Hotel Guest**
Charlotte saw the women's room service dishes sitting in the hallway, including two mugs with different colored lipstick prints on them.

8. **Women's Intuition**
When Julie kissed her husband, she tasted salt on his skin and realized he had been at the gym.

9. **T-Shirt Trouble**
Sally's doll was wearing a shirt that was even smaller than the one she was wearing. Susan knew that both shirts had shrunk, and because Sally was wearing the larger of the two shirts, it must have been her own.

10. **The Missing Socks**
Each day after school, Brian patiently sat and watched the laundry drying on the clothesline. Eventually he saw a bird fly down and snatch a brightly colored sock. Sure enough, Brian found a bird's nest nearby, fabricated of his missing socks.

11. **The Deductive Neighbor**
During the winter, when her neighbors were in town, they kept a fire going to heat the house. Carrie could see smoke coming from the chimney when they were home.

12. Lost and Found

Brad vacuumed the entire house and then checked the vacuum bag. Sure enough, the diamond was right where he thought it would end up.

13. The Hotel Thief

The hotel thief was a pack rat. The hotel management didn't want the reputation of the hotel to be diminished by the presence of rats and figured that because the crime spree was over, things would get back to normal.

14. Filthy Rich

The wallet is full of yen, so Lucas takes the wallet to the Japanese embassy, who will be able to find the rightful owner.

SLEEP ON IT

15. The Early Bird

Knowing he would be exceptionally tired the next morning, Mr. Baxter set up his automated coffeemaker to brew at the designated time. When his alarm failed to wake him, the smell of the coffee brewing did the trick.

16. The Failed Prank

Ben woke up to the radio alarm, which was actually the voice of the DJ announcing the true time.

17. Siesta and Fiesta

Lisa filled her teakettle with water and put it on the burner. Fifteen minutes later the whistling woke her up in time for her tea party with her friends.

18. **Unfamiliar Surroundings**

Sam woke up in a strange bed in a room he didn't immediately recognize, but after seeing the Gideon Bible on the nightstand, he remembered he was in a hotel.

19. **New Year's News**

After winning the New Year's Day Community Marathon, Jason went home to take a nap because he was so tired from staying up all night. He may have been tired, but the evening paper with his winning achievement was enough to get him off the couch.

20. **Sheepless in Seattle**

George was counting how many seconds passed between claps of thunder and flashes of lightning. The thunder and lightning kept him from falling asleep.

21. **Rise and Shine...or Not**

Ryan had spent the entire night reading in bed and set his alarm clock to go off at 5:00 a.m. to remind him to at least get a couple hours of sleep before he had to be at school.

CALL ME WITH THE ANSWER

22. **First Date**

Kati had lost her voice yelling at the football game, so she couldn't talk on the phone.

23. **Unknown Caller**

Rex works for the phone company. Just as he finished repairing a pay phone, it began to ring. The person calling explained that a friend was supposed to be there to receive this call. Rex wrote down a message and posted it in the phone booth.

24. Seven Digits

Jared was house-sitting for his friend. When he called home to talk to his mom, the friend's phone number showed up on his mom's caller ID.

25. What Is Your Emergency?

Susan called her friend from work but forgot to dial 9 to make an outgoing call. The phone number she was trying to dial was 991-1XXX, and by accidentally not dialing enough 9s, she was connected to 911 emergency services.

26. Whom Shall I Say Is Calling?

The woman's daughter had been put up for adoption at birth and was calling her birthmother years later.

CRIMINAL PUZZLEMENT

27. A Dog's Life

Billy was taking a bag of garbage out to the curb in the morning before he left for school.

28. The Intruder

Jennifer knew an intruder was in her home because the chain lock had been fastened on the inside of the door.

29. In for Questioning

Years ago, after serving time for bank robbery, Sammy decided to turn legit. Now he was a police officer interrogating a suspect, not a suspect being interrogated. He had threatened to use his connections in the police force, and he was pleased because he'd managed to get the crook to confess to robbing the bank.

30. **The Tidy Crook**

The crook stole a family heirloom and left a ransom note in its place. He left the house in the exact same condition he found it in, and the victims of the crime didn't realize they had been robbed.

31. **The Witty Cop**

Wesley told the man he could go if he could tell him what radio stations were programmed into his presets (without checking first, of course).

32. **Robbed Again?**

The construction on Nathan's new house isn't finished, so burglars can easily walk right in and take tools, building materials, and appliances, but he knows that as soon as the walls are finished the robberies will end.

33. **Sixth Sense**

Ben is severely allergic to the perfume his assistant is wearing. Even though he can't smell the perfume, it causes his allergies to flare up.

34. **The Unsafe Safe**

Mr. Dunson realized that maybe the contents of his wall safe were not at risk, but the priceless painting hanging in front of it was. He was correct. The painting had been stolen.

35. **The Cheap Fix**

The man bought a hider for a spare key. He was tired of paying the locksmith to get into his car when he locked his keys in.

36. **Joy Ride**

Jim and his friends were riding in a boat that was being pulled down the freeway on a boat trailer.

37. Quick Thinking

Benjamin "accidentally" knocks over the imitation goblets while cleaning and is fired for his incompetence. No one ever suspects that the shattered glass is anything but the original crystal.

38. Above the Law?

The celebrity would wear a novelty mask of himself while robbing the bank.

39. Autograph Snatcher

The man sawed a cast off the boy's arm.

40. Not So Safe

The safe needed a key to open it and not a combination. The thief found the key.

FOR THE ROAD

41. Homeward Bound

Kimmy's parents had been too busy to take their Christmas lights down after the holidays, so they turned them on for Kimmy.

42. Running on Empty

After filling up his tank, Robert drove straight home to get started on dinner. Sadly, before he could finish barbecuing, he ran out of propane!

43. Stuck in Traffic

Joe works in road construction and operates the large trucks.

44. Choosing Sides
Austin lives in England. He drove to work on the right (correct) side of the road, which happened to be the left-hand side.

45. Weather to Forget
During the winter, when the top is up, she sets things on top of the car while she unlocks the door and often forgets them on the roof. During the summer, when the top is down, she sets her things inside the car before she gets in.

46. Seeing Is Believing
The man lost his sunglasses, so he needed to pull over and wait for the sun to set before he could drive safely. He was driving west, directly into the sun, so the light blinded him.

47. Pulled Over for No Reason?
It was getting dark, so the police officer turned on his headlights.

48. The New Sound System
Adam listens to loud music on his headphones to block out the maddening repetitive melody that continually plays over the stereo system in his ice cream truck.

49. Fast Food Freakishness
The man's car is right-hand drive, which makes it hard to make the order and pick up the food in the drive-through. When he has company, he uses the drive-through and his passenger makes the order and takes the food.

50. Windshield Wipers Won't Work?
The woman and her car are going through a car wash.

51. **Green Light, Red Light**

As Kevin approaches the intersection, the traffic light appears to go from red to yellow to green. He knows that yellow usually precedes red, so he stops to be cautious.

52. **Locked Road**

The forest ranger locked the gate open so that no one would close it.

53. **The Long Way Home**

The man was playing his favorite video game at home.

FOR A PRICE

54. **The Inheritance**

Bob's great-great-aunt died in the same fire that burned down her mansion and destroyed all her belongings. To make matters worse, nothing was insured.

55. **The Costly Item**

Shannon bought a lottery ticket and won. She had to pay thousands in taxes.

56. **Two of a Kind**

The music boxes were visually identical, but they played different songs. The woman bought the one she preferred.

57. **Buyer's Remorse**

Tim bought what he thought was a very rare statue that was identical to one he already owned. When he got home to add it to his collection, he realized his statue had been stolen. He'd just spent a fortune buying back his own statue.

58. **The Right Bank**

James knew any bank would be better than his piggy bank.

59. **The Rare Book**

Every time the man opens up his checkbook and writes a check, he lowers his bank balance.

60. **One Person's Junk...**

Derek was trying to sell things that other members of his family wanted to keep, so they quickly put their stuff back inside.

61. **Underpaid?**

He only works 35 hours a week. The man has two part-time jobs in two different time zones. He works from 8:00 a.m. to 12:00 p.m., takes an hour lunch break to drive to his second job, and works from 2:00 p.m. to 5:00 p.m.

PUZZLING BEHAVIOR

62. **Is It a Miracle?**

The men were ice fishing.

63. **Always Be Prepared**

Brian is a commercial airline pilot. He usually flies at around 30,000 feet, or six miles above sea level. Life jackets are required in case of an emergency water landing.

64. **Scared Silly**

Suzie's pet rat had recently escaped from its cage. After being startled by it in the basement, she quickly disposed of the mousetraps so it wouldn't hurt itself.

65. If the Shoe Fits

Jenny's favorite earrings are a pair of tiny gold tennis shoes.

66. Trouble at Work

Karl works at a movie theater. He took his family to a movie on his day off. The movie was so horrible they ended up leaving early.

67. That's Unheard Of

The man wears headphones as a visual cue to let people know that he can't hear them. People will get his attention before they start talking to him, and he can read their lips. They never have to even know he is deaf.

68. A Passing Failure

The student wrote a research paper on Leonardo da Vinci for her history class. She wrote the paper using "mirror writing"—writing backward from right to left. Leonardo wrote this way in his notebooks to avoid the theft of his ideas. When the teacher initially saw the paper, she assumed it was gibberish and gave the student an F. But when the student told her to use a mirror to read it, she changed the grade and gave her extra credit for her cleverness.

69. No Mulligan?

A sudden storm dumped golf-ball-sized hail across the whole course.

70. For Sale Fib

He wants his neighbors to think he is moving so they will return the things they borrowed.

71. Sudden Outburst

Leslie's grandfather clock struck noon.

72. **What Not to Do**
Sam and Devin are brothers who share a room. Sam talks in his sleep.

73. **The Forgotten Gift**
Kevin was celebrating his own birthday party at the pizza parlor. Afterward, Kevin was going to his friend Tim's house for his birthday party.

CLEVER THINKERS

74. **A Needle in a Haystack**
Mrs. Riley had a bright idea when she saw the horse trough. She tossed the straw into the water and moved it around until the pin sank to the bottom.

75. **A Key Solution**
Betty attached a spare house key to her dog's favorite toy and left it in the house. After her run, she told her dog to go fetch his toy. Her dog entered the house through the doggy door and returned with the toy and key.

76. **Who's There?**
She put a sign on the doorbell that said Out of Order, but her friends and family knew that it still worked. She knew that whoever knocked was an unwanted visitor.

77. **It's Not Polite to Stare**
Prior to the staring competitions, Sam puts plugs in his nose and covers his clothing with pepper. His opponent gets pepper up his nose and sneezes, momentarily closing his eyes.

78. **All in a Name**
Sharon has a unique heart tattoo on her shoulder with the

name Aaron. Meagan saw a man with an identical tattoo but with the name Sharon and knew they must be a couple.

PUZZLING SITUATIONS

79. **The New Girl**
The girl was visiting her twin sister.

80. **Teacher's Pet**
The girl is homeschooled.

81. **Special Delivery**
Jack was not expecting to get caught but eventually he was sent to jail for mail theft.

82. **Playing Hooky**
Carl didn't get fired because he was still doing his job. He is the bodyguard of his employer's daughter. The daughter, on the other hand, got in trouble for skipping the important business meeting.

83. **All Trick and No Treat**
Susan's porch light burned out, so kids didn't come trick-or-treating. Being blind, she didn't notice the light go out. She was reading a book written in Braille.

84. **Blind Date**
Hannah went to the bank where Harold works to meet him for lunch. Harold, as a security guard, spent his day monitoring the security cameras and therefore could see everyone who entered the bank. Unfortunately, the description Hannah gave Harold was of the color of her clothing. Harold was not able to distinguish who she was on the black-and-white monitors.

85. **The Invisible Girl**
Carly hid in the girl's bathroom.

86. **More or Less?**
A flame. You blow on a candle to put it out and you blow on a campfire to help it grow.

87. **Fleeting Interest**
Frank's wife had returned a book to the library that he had recently finished. To his dismay, she hadn't noticed the $100 bill he was using as a bookmark.

88. **Art for the Ages**
Jane got a tattoo.

89. **Losing with Style**
Charles was running in a relay race. He was the fastest runner, but his team came in second.

90. **Mirror, Mirror**
You won't see your reflection when you look in (or inside) a bathroom mirror cabinet.

91. **Puzzle Puzzle**
Simon assembled the backside of the jigsaw puzzle, which was completely blank. He couldn't see the image until he flipped the completed puzzle over.

92. **Artistic License**
The woman paints a picture of her identical twin sister.

93. **The House Painter**
Jim became an artist and started painting pictures of houses.

94. **Water Rules**
Two or more people must ride in a car while driving in the carpool lane.

95. **Lucky Bug**
The woman thought he was winking at her.

96. **Power Outage**
The man lives in the country where the electricity frequently goes out. He uses propane to light his home, to cook, and to heat his water. His radio is battery powered, and his fireplace provides sufficient heat.

97. **A Case of Amnesia?**
James was born.

98. **Good Advice**
His friend told him to give up gambling. He'd been losing his stuff while playing poker with his friends.

Alternate answer: His friend tells him to get rid of all his stuff and become a monk. He would no longer misplace his things because he wouldn't own anything!

99. **Bad Hair Day**
For the past ten years, James has shaved his head with a razor, but when he tries growing it out, he realizes he can't because he is bald.

100. **When It Rains, It Pours**
Tom Baker owns a convertible. It was sunny the day before and the top was down so he merely reached into his car and grabbed the keys.

The Awesome Book of
One-Minute Mysteries and Brain Teasers

Mind-Boggling One-Minute Mysteries
and Brain Teasers

Because so many folks have enjoyed this first book of mysteries and brain teasers, award-winning author Sandy Silverthorne and John Warner have created more (and better!) mysteries for super-sleuths of all ages—two more books for the whole family.

Each mystery is complete with helpful clues, comic-strip-style illustrations, and solutions. If you're baffled after reading the first clue, you can read another, one by one until that "aha moment" finally arrives. Sure to make you scratch your head, think outside the box, and chuckle all the while, these are the perfect books to pass the time or pep up a party—good clean fun for anytime, anywhere, and anyone!

More Great Harvest House Books
by Sandy Silverthorne

The Awesome Book About God for Kids

In the Bible, God not only tells you what He is like—He *shows* you. The Bible is full of action-packed stories that reveal God's nature as He works behind the scenes. Now you can read many of these stories in up-to-date language with some fun twists and hilarious cartoons.

The Awesome Book of Unusual Bible Heroes for Kids

The heroes of the Bible aren't always the biggest, strongest, smartest, or most popular people. In fact, as you're about to see, God seems to prefer to do amazing things through people who simply are willing to follow Him.

Who knows what special assignment God might have for you! These Bible stories, which include some fun modern-day twists and hilarious cartoons, show that when you look to God for direction and help, He can do wonderful things in your life.

The Awesome Book of Bible Stories for Kids

The Bible is full of amazing real-life stories. But they happened so long ago—do they really apply to your life today?

Yes, they do! God's message to you never gets old. So use your imagination...what if the stories in the Bible happened in your house or at your school? What if Joshua's battle at Jericho inspired a video game? What if Gideon competed on a game show? What if Jesus sent you a text message? How cool would that be!

These short Bible stories in high-tech settings are great fun, and they reveal the awesome truths and exciting promises God wants to share with you today.

101 Awesome Bible Facts for Kids

Does the Bible sometimes seem hard to understand? No wonder—it was written a *long* time ago in a faraway part of the world. But never fear! This little book is filled with one-page tantalizing tidbits and intriguing items (complete with hilarious cartoons) that will make you feel right at home in the world of the Bible and help you understand God's message to you.